I0813554

NFL RIVALRIES

FALCONS VS. SAINTS

By Amy C. Rea

Kaleidoscope
Minneapolis, MN

Your Front Row Seat to the Games

This edition first published in 2020 by Kaleidoscope Publishing, Inc.

For information regarding permission, write to
Kaleidoscope Publishing, Inc.
6012 Blue Circle Drive
Minnetonka, MN 55343

Library of Congress Control Number
2019939218

ISBN
978-1-64519-082-0 (library bound)
978-1-64494-167-6 (paperback)
978-1-64519-183-4 (ebook)

Printed in the United States of America.

TABLE OF CONTENTS

CHAPTER 1

A Hot Day in Atlanta

September 23, 2018, was a hot fall day in Atlanta. The action inside the stadium was even hotter. Almost 75,000 people filled the seats. They were ready for a big game. The Atlanta Falcons were hosting the New Orleans Saints.

Both teams had great quarterbacks. Both could also put up big scores. That showed early.

Saints quarterback Drew Brees dropped back to pass. Wide receiver Ted Ginn was open. He caught the pass. Then he ran it in for a touchdown. The visiting Saints fans roared approval. Their team led 7–0.

Atlanta's new Mercedes-Benz Stadium opened in 2017.

Saints quarterback Drew Brees prepares to pass against the Falcons.

The lead didn't last long. Soon Matt Ryan struck. The Falcons quarterback passed. Wide receiver Calvin Ridley caught it. Touchdown! The game was tied.

The Saints answered. They scored two field goals. Then Ridley was back. He scored another touchdown for the Falcons. That put them one point ahead.

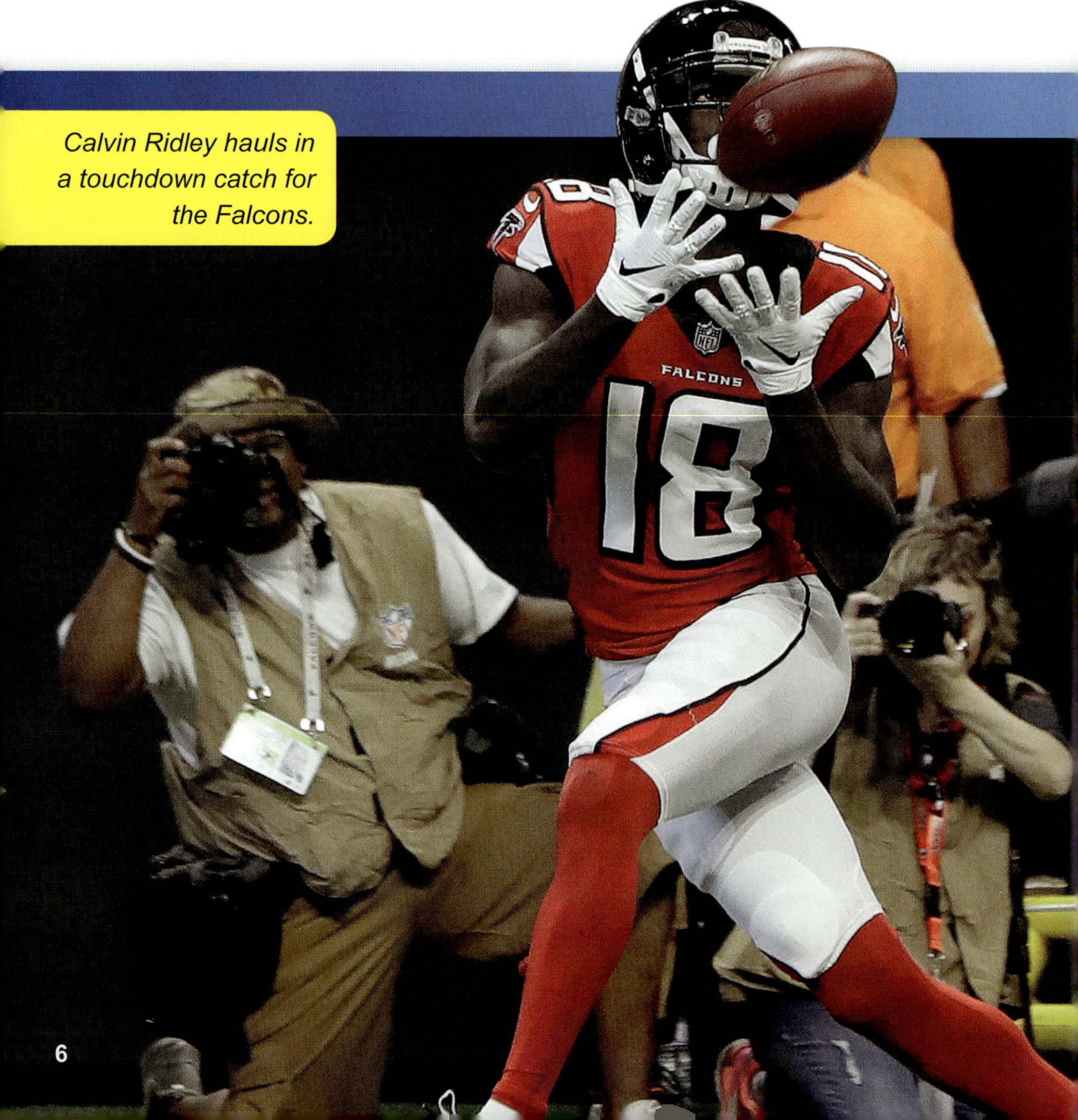

Calvin Ridley hauls in a touchdown catch for the Falcons.

Only six seconds remained in the first half. The Saints scored another field goal. They took a 16–14 lead into the half.

FUN FACT

Calvin Ridley set a team rookie record by scoring ten touchdowns in 2018.

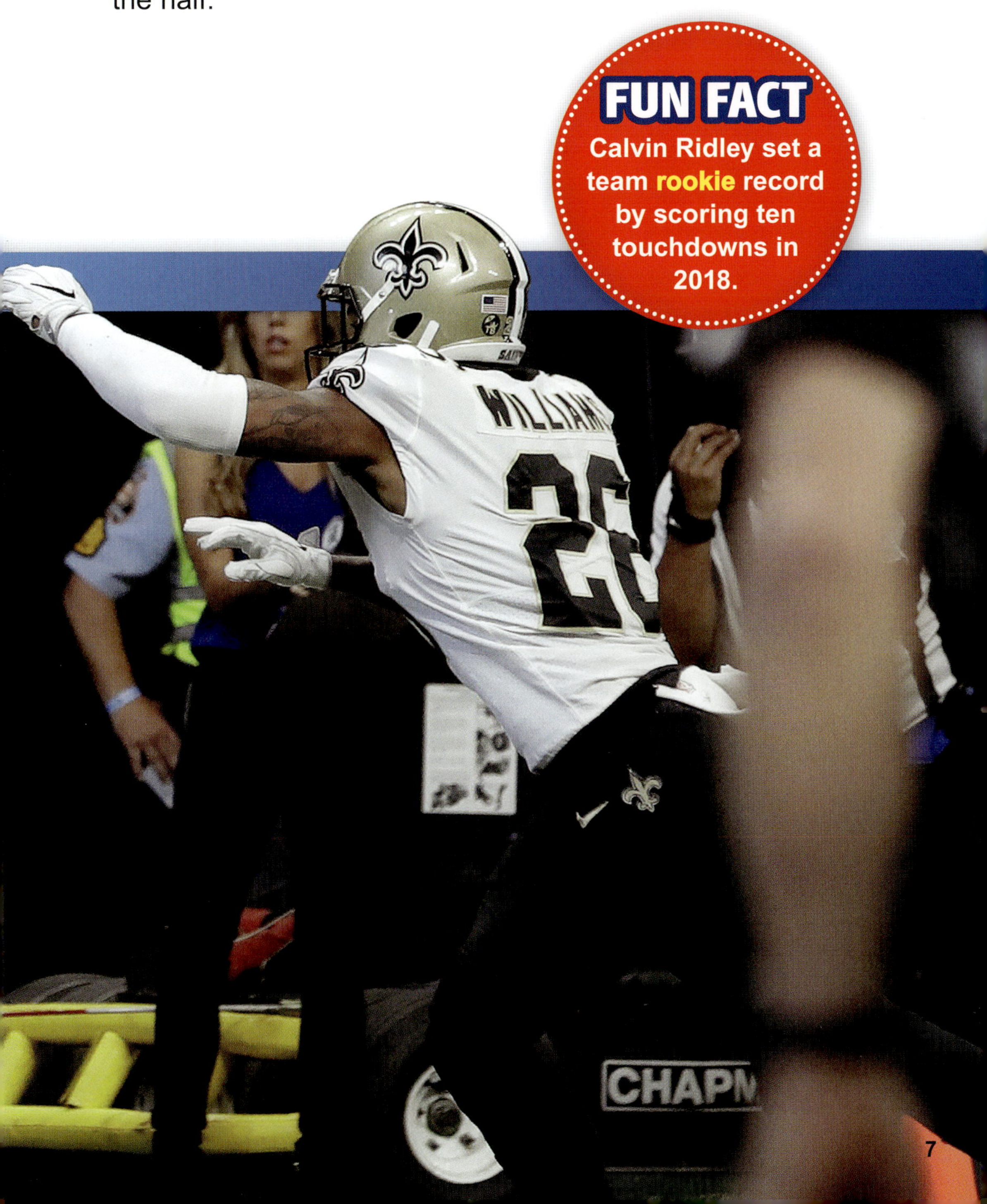

Both teams continued to score. Ridley caught another touchdown pass. Then Brees threw one. The Saints still led by two. This continued in the fourth quarter. Atlanta scored. New Orleans answered. Then Atlanta scored again. The Falcons added a **two-point conversion**. But the Saints were not done. They tied the game. It was on to **overtime**.

The teams had ten minutes to break the tie. Now the defenses stepped up. Seven minutes went by. Finally, Brees ended it. He ran one yard for a touchdown. The Saints won! A thrilling rivalry continued.

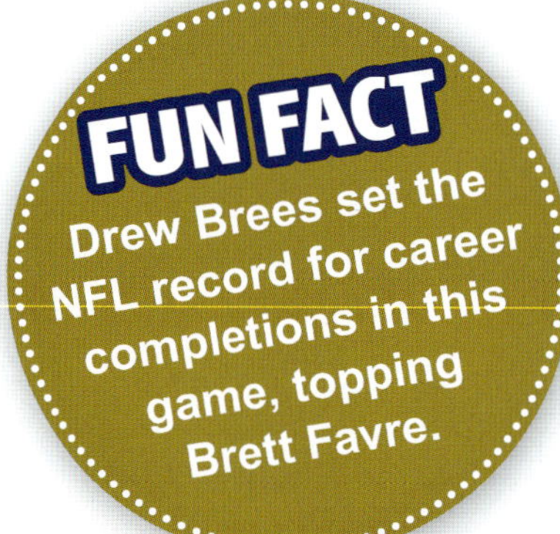

OVERTIME

The NFL did not always allow overtime. Games originally ended in ties. Overtime began in 1974. At first, overtime was 15 minutes. It was like a fifth quarter. In 2017, it was shortened to 10 minutes.

Brees dives over his offensive line for the winning touchdown against the Falcons.

CHAPTER 2

The Rivalry Starts and Grows

The Falcons were bad. The Saints were worse. That didn't matter to 83,437 fans. They crowded into the stadium. A rivalry was beginning.

The Falcons formed in 1966. The Saints followed in 1967. Both were brand new.

They were the league's first Southeastern teams. On November 26, 1967, they played in New Orleans. It was their first meeting. Atlanta was 1–8–1. New Orleans was 1–9. But bragging rights were on the line. The players were **aggressive**. They hit each other hard. Both sides felt they got incorrect calls. In the end, the Saints won 27–24.

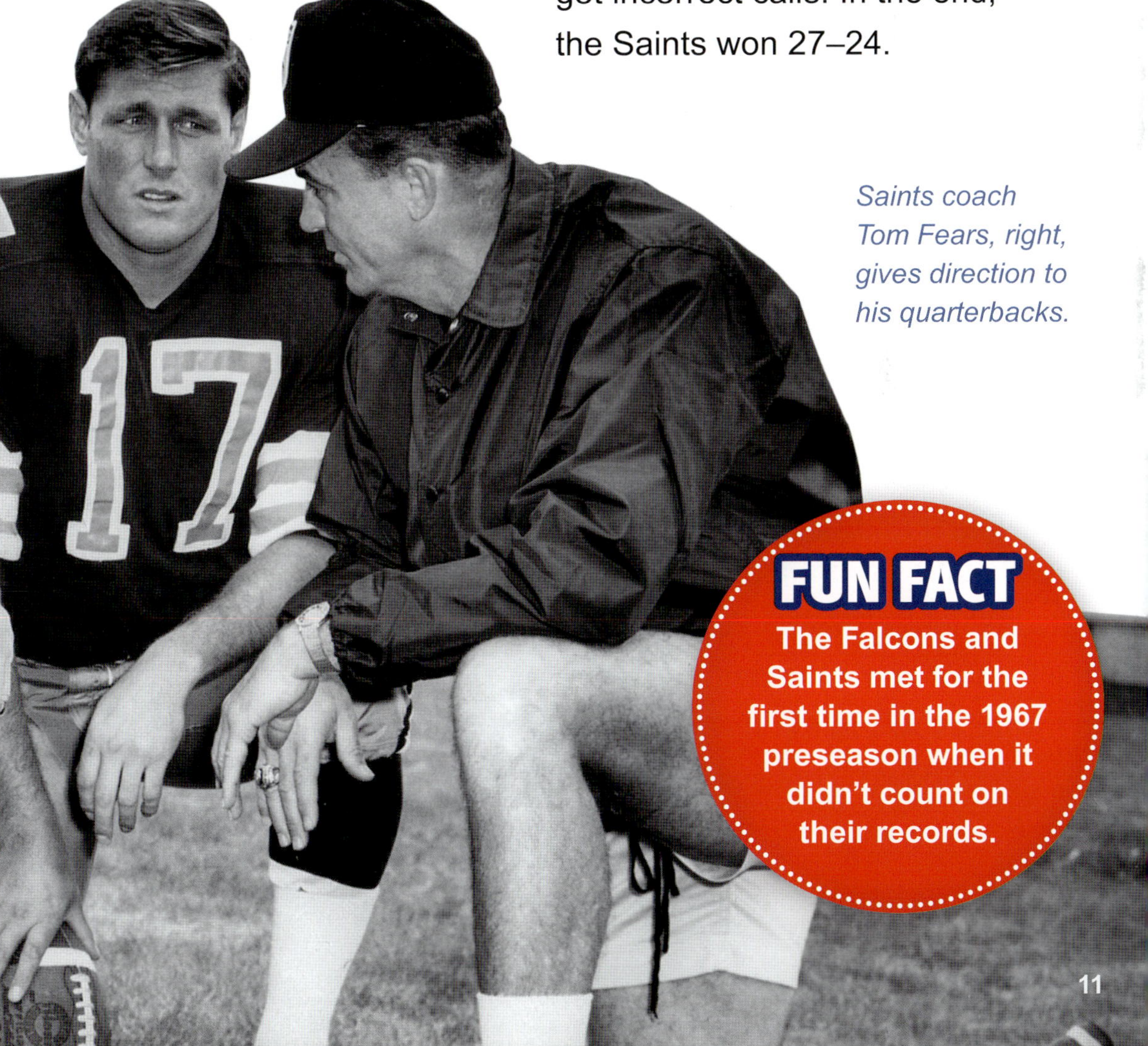

Saints coach Tom Fears, right, gives direction to his quarterbacks.

FUN FACT

The Falcons and Saints met for the first time in the 1967 preseason when it didn't count on their records.

SWITCHING SIDES

When the Saints needed a first head coach, they selected Tom Fears. He had been a Hall of Famer as a player. He also knew a thing or two about the Saints' new rival. Fears had been an assistant in Atlanta the year before.

The Saints and Falcons play twice every year. They have since 1970. That is when they joined the same **division**. At first, neither team was very good. But both had strong 1991 seasons. On December 28 of that year, they met a third time. This marked their first meeting in the playoffs.

The Saints hosted. They led by three at halftime. Both sides were fighting hard. The game remained close. Finally, Atlanta broke free. Wide receiver Michael Haynes caught a pass around midfield. He turned upfield. He outran one defender. Then he outran two more. It was a 61-yard touchdown. That sealed a 27–20 Falcons victory.

MICHAEL HAYNES

TO THE HOUSE

The Falcons lined up at their own 39-yard line. They needed a score to break the 20–20 tie against the Saints. Quarterback Chris Miller dropped back. He threw a short pass to Michael Haynes out to the right. Haynes then beat his defender and took off. Two Saints chased after him. They had no chance. Haynes sprinted to the end zone for a 61-yard touchdown. The Falcons won 27–20 to advance in the playoffs.

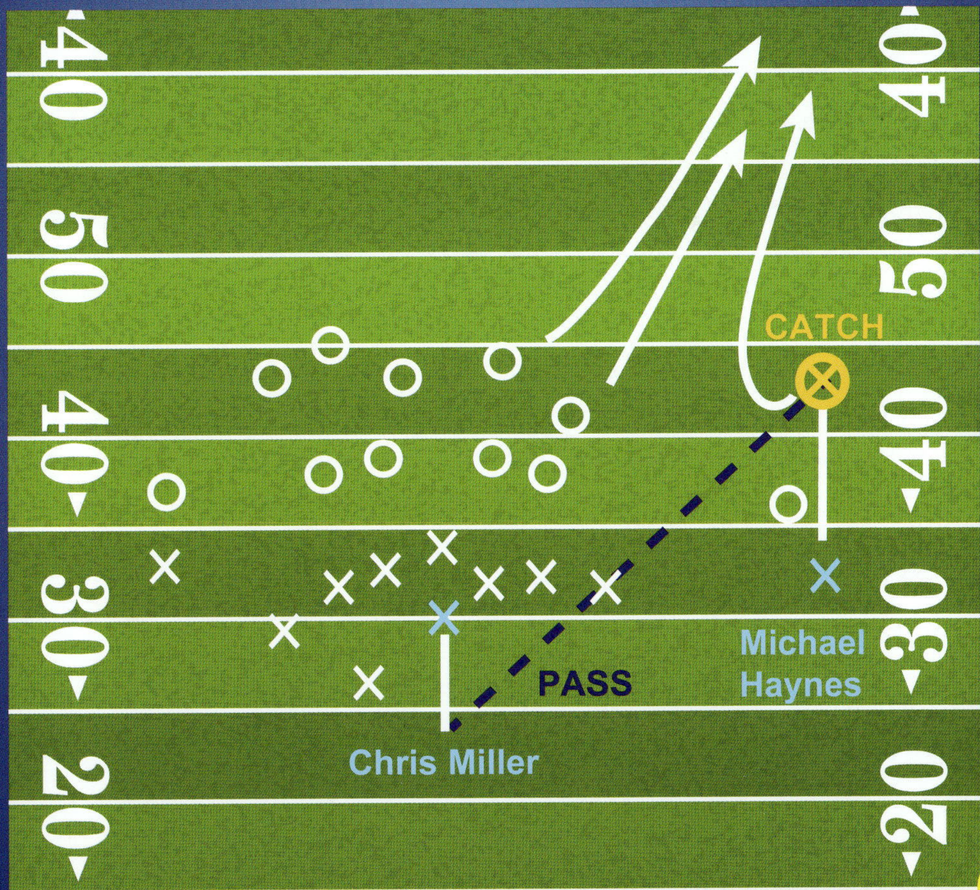

HEAD TO HEAD

STATS

Through the 2018 season

ATLANTA		NEW ORLEANS
51	WINS	48
51.5	WINNING PERCENTAGE	48.5
2,200	POINTS SCORED	2,099
1	PLAYOFF WINS	0
10 (1995–99)	LONGEST WIN STREAK	(1986–89) 6
0	TOTAL SUPER BOWL VICTORIES	1

The 1998 Falcons reached the Super Bowl. It was their first. The Saints continued to struggle. In 2006, that changed. The team had played 39 seasons. It reached the playoffs just five times. Then Drew Brees arrived. The quarterback turned things around. The Saints became a power. The 2009 Saints even won the Super Bowl.

Atlanta had to keep up. Matt Ryan made sure it did. He was just a rookie quarterback in 2008. But he started every game. The Falcons even made the playoffs. Now both teams were really good. The rivalry heated up, too. Between 2006 and 2018, their division crowned thirteen champions. The Falcons or Saints won eight times.

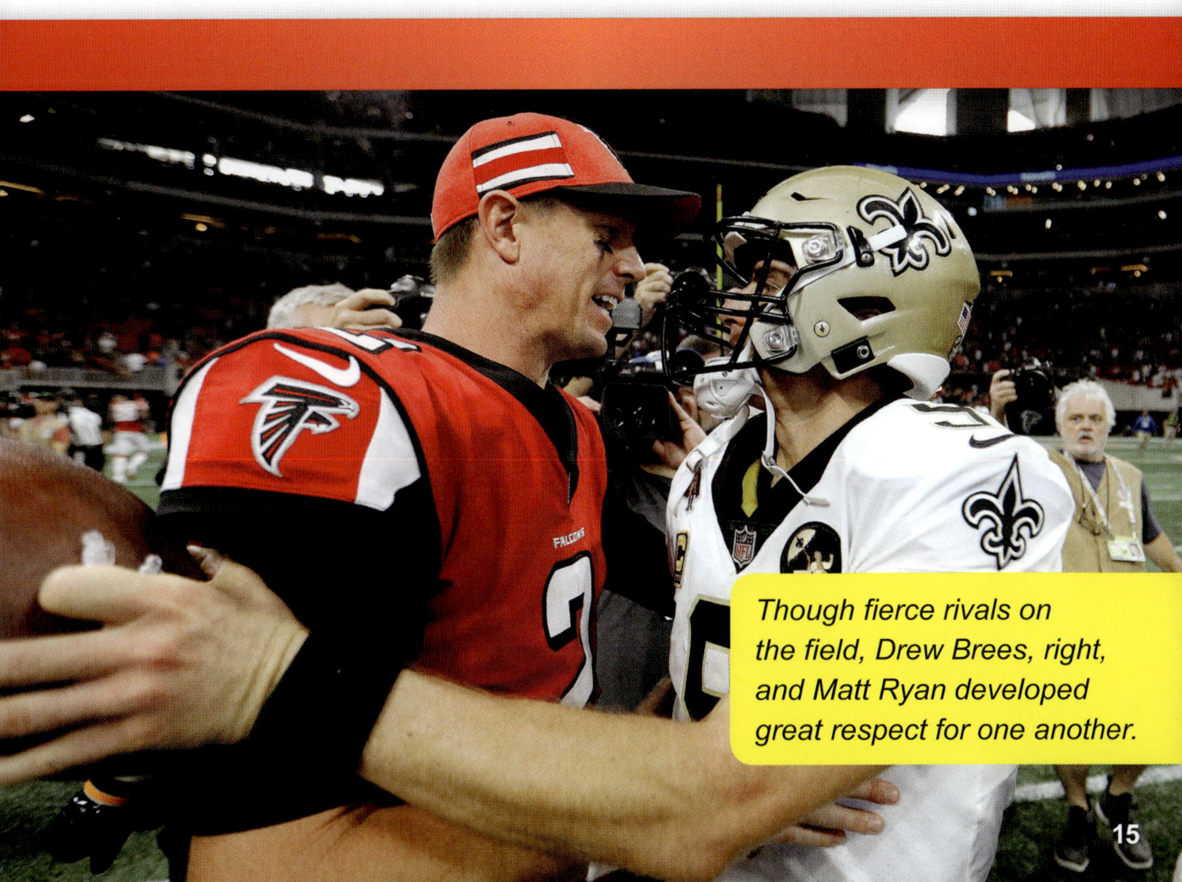

Though fierce rivals on the field, Drew Brees, right, and Matt Ryan developed great respect for one another.

CHAPTER 3

Archie Manning was a bright spot for the Saints during the 1970s and early 1980s.

Legendary Players

The game wasn't going well for the Saints. It was November 1977. The Falcons were in town. And they led 20–7 at the half. Then Archie Manning got hot. The Saints quarterback dropped back. He found tight end Henry Childs. Touchdown! But New Orleans still trailed. No problem. In the fourth quarter, Manning found Childs again. Another touchdown! New Orleans came back to win 21–20.

The Saints didn't win much in the 1970s. But Manning was a star. He joined the team in 1971. He left in 1982. Manning passed for 21,734 yards. He added 115 touchdown passes. Both stats are still among the best in team history.

FUN FACT

Archie Manning's sons, Peyton and Eli Manning, grew up to be Super Bowl–winning quarterbacks in the 2000s.

In 1989, the ball landed in Deion Sanders's arms. He took off running. It was a punt return. And the Falcons rookie went 68 yards. Touchdown! Not a bad start to his NFL career. Sanders joined the Falcons that year. "Neon Deion" was flashy. He was also really good. Sanders played cornerback. But he also was dangerous as a return man. Sanders played five years in Atlanta.

Offensive linemen don't get as much attention. But the Saints' Willie Roaf was one of the best. He played in New Orleans from 1993 to 2001. Roaf made the Pro Bowl seven times with the Saints.

It took a special effort for defenders to get around the Saints' Willie Roaf.

Playing on all sides of the ball, Deion Sanders scored ten touchdowns in five seasons for the Falcons.

FUN FACT

Deion Sanders is the only person to have played in both the Super Bowl and the World Series.

Since 2006, good quarterbacks and offenses have been central to the Falcons–Saints rivalry. Drew Brees is six feet tall. That is short for an NFL quarterback. But he has a strong arm. The Saints signed him in 2006. He became one of the game's greatest passers. By 2018, he had played the Falcons 27 times. Brees helped the Saints win 18 of those games.

Matt Ryan and Julio Jones helped the Falcons keep up. Ryan, a quarterback, arrived in 2008. Wide receiver Jones followed three years later. Together they are dominant. That showed on October 2, 2016. Ryan passed for more than 500 yards. Jones had more than 300 receiving yards. No other teammates in NFL history had achieved that in one game.

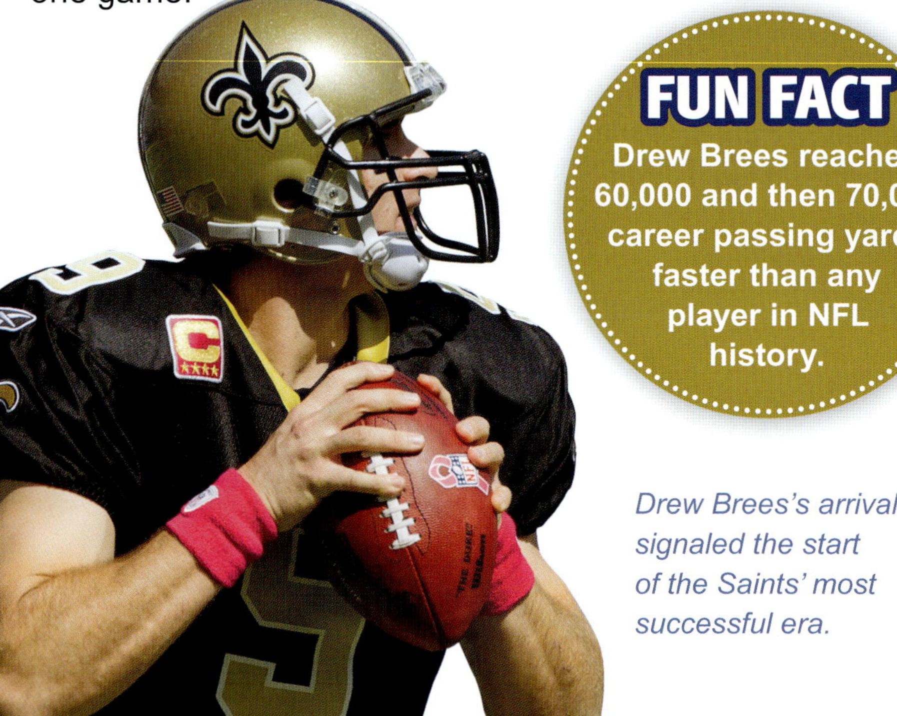

FUN FACT

Drew Brees reached 60,000 and then 70,000 career passing yards faster than any player in NFL history.

Drew Brees's arrival signaled the start of the Saints' most successful era.

Falcons receiver Julio Jones uses his size and strength to dominate opponents.

CHAPTER 4

Falcons Fans, Saints Fans

NFL leaders looked at a map. The league had a gap. It had teams on the East Coast. Teams played in the Midwest. Some were on the West Coast, too. But none were from the Southeast. The Falcons changed that. They **debuted** in 1966. The Saints followed in 1967.

Their rivalry was natural. The cities are only 470 miles (756 km) apart. Fans can make that drive in seven hours. And they often do. Their support has only gotten stronger as the teams improved over the years.

FUN FACT

The Falcons have a special **chant**: "Rise Up." Fans bring giant banners with these two words to wave at games.

Falcons fans cheer on their team.

Rivalry Map

Wisconsin
Michigan
Iowa
Ohio
Illinois
Indiana
West Virginia
Missouri
Kentucky
Virginia
North Carolina
Tennessee
South Carolina
Arkansas
Alabama
Mississippi
Atlanta Falcons
Mercedes-Benz Stadium
Atlanta, Georgia
Louisiana
Georgia
Florida
New Orleans Saints
Mercedes-Benz Superdome
New Orleans, Louisiana
N
W
E
S

Drew Brees raises his arm high. Then he drops it. The crowd of 70,000 Saints fans is ready. "Who Dat?!" they yell. The chant dates back to the 1970s. Saints fans began using it in 1983. It became a popular rallying cry. Brees helped make it a **tradition** in 2010. A special guest comes onto the field. The referee tosses the coin. Then the guest signals to the fans. They respond with the chant.

The Saints fans are very loud. Sometimes players struggle to hear their coaches. In 2019, the noise caused vibrations. This resulted in damage to their stadium.

The Superdome in New Orleans is known for having some of the NFL's rowdiest fans.

FUN FACT
Saints fans call themselves "Who Dat Nation."

Jamal Anderson made sure Falcons fans had plenty to cheer about in 1998.

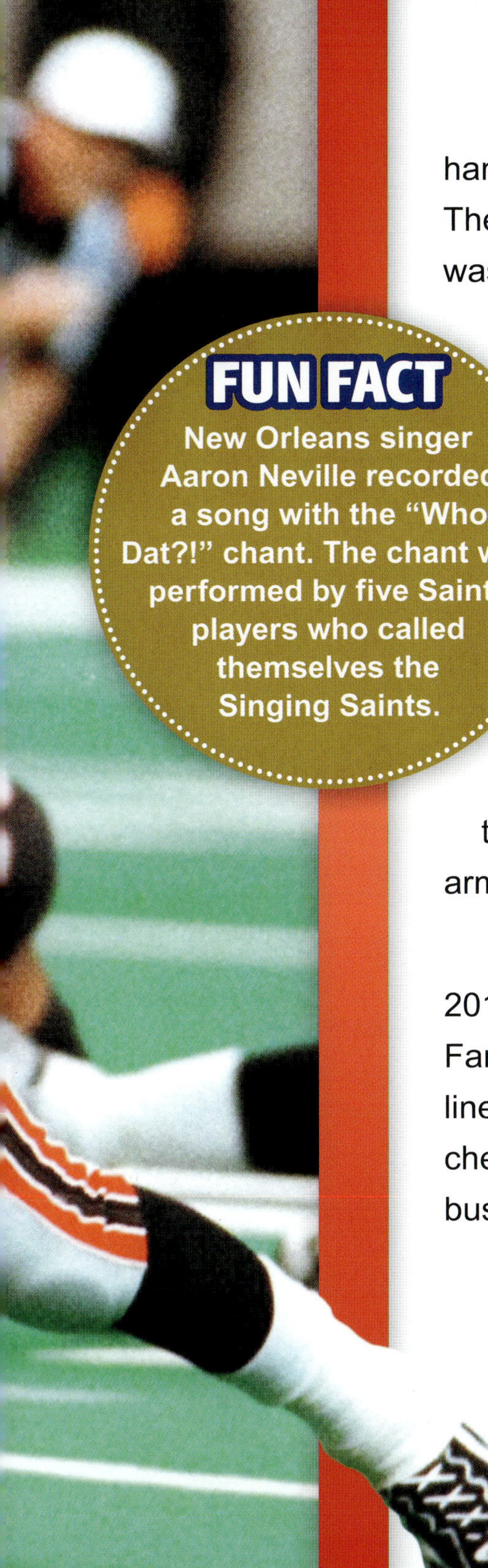

FUN FACT
New Orleans singer Aaron Neville recorded a song with the "Who Dat?!" chant. The chant was performed by five Saints players who called themselves the Singing Saints.

In 1998, Jamal Anderson took the handoff. The running back cut left. Then he raced into the end zone. It was another Falcons touchdown. The fans rose to their feet. They knew what was coming. It was time for the "Dirty Bird." The Falcons struggled in their early years. But they were really good that year. They became really popular, too. Anderson and the "Dirty Bird" played a big role. He performed the dance after touchdowns. It involves flapping arms like an excited falcon.

Falcons fans are **devoted**. The 2016 team reached the Super Bowl. Fans saw the players off. Supporters lined both sides of the streets. They cheered and waved signs as the team buses went by.

Fans in both Atlanta and New Orleans love their teams. Without the fans, the rivalry would be much less exciting.

BEYOND THE BOOK

After reading the book, it's time to think about what you learned. Try the following exercises to jumpstart your ideas.

THINK

THAT'S NEWS TO ME. In 2016, the Falcons' Matt Ryan and Julio Jones became the first pair in NFL history to be a 500-yard passer and 300-yard receiver in the same game. How could news sources provide more information on that? What new things could you find? Where could you go to find those news sources?

CREATE

PRIMARY SOURCES. There are many kinds of primary sources for football information. These are resources that have direct, or first-hand, information about the players and games. Create a list of the kinds of primary sources you could find on the Falcons–Saints rivalry.

SHARE

SUM IT UP. Write a paragraph summarizing the important points from this book. Write it in your own words. Do not just copy what is in the book. Then share the paragraph with a classmate. What feedback or questions does that classmate have?

GROW

REAL-LIFE RESEARCH. What kind of real-world places could you visit to do more research about the Falcons–Saints rivalry? What other topics could you learn about at these places?

Visit www.ninjaresearcher.com/0820 to learn how to take your research skills and book report writing to the next level!

RESEARCH

SEARCH LIKE A PRO
Learn about how to use search engines to find useful websites.

FACT OR FAKE?
Discover how you can tell a trusted website from an untrustworthy resource.

TEXT DETECTIVE
Explore how to zero in on the information you need most.

SHOW YOUR WORK
Research responsibly—learn how to cite sources.

WRITE

GET TO THE POINT
Learn how to express your main ideas.

PLAN OF ATTACK
Learn prewriting exercises and create an outline.

DOWNLOADABLE REPORT FORMS

Further Resources

BOOKS

Bates, Greg. *Matt Ryan: Football Star*. Focus Readers, 2018.

Scheff, Matt. *Fierce NFL Rivalries: 12 Super-Charged Matchups*. 12-Story Library, 2016.

Whiting, Jim. *The Story of the New Orleans Saints*. Creative Education, 2019.

WEBSITES

Factsurfer.com gives you a safe, fun way to find more information.

1. Go to www.factsurfer.com.
2. Enter “Falcons vs. Saints” into the search box and click 🔍.
3. Select your book cover to see a list of related websites.

Glossary

aggressive: To be aggressive means one is being forceful in trying to overpower an opponent. The Saints and Falcons players were aggressive in their first game.

chant: A chant is something groups of people yell over and over again. Saints fans are famous for their "Who Dat?!" chant.

debut: To debut is to make one's first appearance. The Falcons made their NFL debut in 1966.

devoted: Being devoted means having a strong loyalty for a person or object. Falcons and Saints fans are both devoted to their teams.

division: A division is a group of teams that regularly play games against each other. The Falcons and Saints have been in the same division since 1970.

overtime: Overtime is an extra period of play to determine a winner if the game is tied after four quarters. The Saints finally beat the Falcons in overtime.

rookie: A rookie is a player in his first season in a new league. Deion Sanders was a star kick returner as a rookie.

tradition: A tradition is something people do over and over again. The "Who Dat?!" chant became a tradition for Saints fans.

two-point conversion: A two-point conversion is when a team successfully gets the ball into the end zone on the play after a touchdown, rather than kicking for one point. The Falcons scored on a two-point conversion to tie the game.

Index

PHOTO CREDITS

The images in this book are reproduced through the courtesy of: Damian Strohmeyer/AP Images, front cover (left); Margaret Bowles/AP Images, front cover (right); EFKS/Shutterstock Images, front cover (background); Jeff Bukowski/Shutterstock Images, p. 3 (left), p. 3 (right); Revel Pix LLC/Shutterstock Images, p. 4; Mark Humphrey/AP Images, pp. 5, 6–7; Dan Thornberg/Shutterstock Images, p. 8; Curtis Compton/Atlanta Journal-Constitution/AP Images, pp. 9, 21; NFL Photos/AP Images, pp. 10–11; enterlinedesign/Shutterstock Images, p. 13; Red Line Editorial, pp. 14, 23; David Goldman/AP Images, p. 15; Al Messerschmidt/AP Images, pp. 16–17, 19; Paul Jasienski/AP Images, p. 18; Action Sports Photography/Shutterstock Images, p. 20; Jamie Lamor Thompson/Shutterstock Images, pp. 22, 30; GagliardiPhotography/Shutterstock Images, p. 24; Aaron M. Sprecher/AP Images, p. 25; Alan Mothner/AP Images, pp. 26–27.

ABOUT THE AUTHOR

Amy C. Rea grew up in northern Minnesota and now lives in a Minneapolis suburb with her husband, two sons, and dog. She writes frequently about traveling around Minnesota.